INNOVATIONS:

A RECREATION THERAPY APPROACH TO RESTORATIVE PROGRAMS

INNOVATIONS:

A RECREATION THERAPY APPROACH TO RESTORATIVE PROGRAMS

DAWN R. DE VRIES, MPA, CTRS
JULIE M. LAKE, CTRS

VENTURE PUBLISHING, INC.
STATE COLLEGE, PA

Venture Publishing, Inc.
1999 Cato Avenue
State College, PA 16801
Phone: (814) 234-4561
Fax: (814) 234-1651

Production Manager: Richard Yocum
Manuscript Editing: Valerie Paukovits

Library of Congress Catalogue Card Number 2001098995
ISBN 1-892132-29-X

Recreation Therapy
is the delivery
of treatment services
to persons with various disabilities
with the purpose
of improving or maintaining
functional abilities
utilizing recreation and leisure
to accomplish
specific goals and objectives
to enhance an individual's
quality of life.

—Dawn De Vries

TABLE OF CONTENTS

INTRODUCTION

Recreation therapy focuses on improving, restoring, and/or maintaining functional and leisure skills and abilities. In long-term care facilities, restorative nursing services also address restoring or maintaining function, particularly range of motion. Both serve long-term care residents by enhancing residents' quality of life.

Recreation therapy is the delivery of treatment services to persons with various disabilities with the purpose of improving or maintaining functional abilities. This is done by utilizing recreation and leisure to accomplish specific goals and objectives to enhance an individual's quality of life. "[Recreation therapy] is one of those professions that by definition is concerned with individuals and how they cope with, adjust to, or compensate for an illness or disability" (Peterson & Gunn, 1984). Furthermore, "recreation therapy reduces the risk of physical complications secondary to disability and improves the general physical and perceptual motor functioning of the disabled, including the elderly" (Russoniello, 1992). Restorative nursing works to accomplish the same goal.

At the same time, restorative nursing assists individuals in adjusting to and compensating for a disability by working to improve functional abilities. Restorative nursing's goal is to help a person to be as independent as possible. This discipline uses various modalities to work on range of motion, mobility, and activities of daily living (ADLs).

The *Innovations* program developed at a Michigan nursing home was designed to integrate these two disciplines into a cooperative program. Recreation therapy and restorative nursing work together to address the residents' needs. The name "Innovations" was selected by the recreation therapy staff because they felt that this program was distinctly different and innovative compared to other recreation therapy or restorative nursing programs.

Developed in the summer and fall of 1998, the program sprung into action in November 1998. To date, the program has proven its value and worth, as it consistently accomplishes its purpose and goals. The Innovations program is provided in addition to the regular recreation therapy program. The mission of the recreation therapy department is:

> to [provide] a variety of opportunities to meet the physical, cognitive, spiritual, creative and psychosocial needs of [the] residents. The use of recreational and therapeutic activities serves to enhance each individual's identity, respect and dignity . . . [The program] seeks to help residents maintain their highest possible functioning level and thus, enhance each resident's quality of life. (Brookcrest Christian Nursing Home, 1997)

Goals for the recreation therapy program include improving or maintaining independence, participating in recreation and leisure, socialization, maintaining physical and cognitive abilities, enhancing self-esteem, and community involvement (Lewis, 1985).

The facility offers a four-track program which involves residents in programs and activities based on their functioning levels and individual needs. *Large group activities*, ranging from 12 to 40+ people, are geared toward those who are cognitively and socially high functioning. These residents participate in groups with minimal to no physical assistance, are socially appropriate, and are cognitively intact or have minimal cognitive deficits. Any resident can participate in these groups but there is a higher resident to staff ratio, meaning little assistance is provided for participation. These groups are provided in a large all-purpose room 365 days a year. The large group program is similar to a typical nursing home activity program.

Small group activities are the second track provided for residents. Small groups occur in the hallway dining rooms and consist of 4–12 residents. With these smaller groups, staff are able to provide one-to-one interventions and cueing needed by individuals with cognitive or emotional impairments. These groups are specifically geared toward those with dementia or those who need individualized attention. Individuals who exhibit behavior problems; need verbal, visual, or tactile cues; are socially inappropriate; or need physical assistance for task completion are placed in this second track.

The third track is aimed at those needing one-to-one visits or *sensory therapy*. Individuals in this track are uninvolved in leisure or group activities due to physical, cognitive, or emotional reasons. Some of these residents receive one-to-one staff or volunteer visits to facilitate socialization. Others who receive sensory therapy tend to be more impaired than those involved in the small group programs. The facility has a specially designed sensory therapy program, which occurs daily to meet the needs of severely impaired residents.

The final track within the recreation therapy program is group *cotreatments*. This program combines recreation therapy treatment with occupational, physical, and speech therapies for individuals receiving skilled treatment on the Medicare A hallway, which is a subacute and general rehabilitation unit. These group cotreatments are aimed at improving functional skills and abilities for individuals suffering from orthopedic impairments, cardiac problems, and strokes. Most of these individuals (approximately 87%) will return to the community or to a lesser level of care, such as an assisted living facility. The Innovations program is an addition to this four-track program. In essence, Innovations provides the fifth track to the recreation therapy services provided within this facility.

This book details the background, development, implementation and evaluation of the Innovations program. The information was first presented at the Michigan Association of Homes and Services for the Aged (MAHSA) Annual Convention in April 1999. Since that presentation, information has been added and clarified, thanks to input and participation from the original audience of 30 people.

PURPOSE AND BACKGROUND

Innovations was designed and established as a "program of therapeutic activities to restore or maintain functional abilities and skills." Developed by the authors of this text, two recreation therapists, it involves the cooperation and support of the leadership staff and the entire interdisciplinary team. The program is also a paradigm shift, involving a change from the traditional restorative program to a new interdisciplinary team approach.

Innovations is a referral-based program. Prior to entering Innovations, residents must be referred by a member of the interdisciplinary team. Any team member can make a referral to the program, which addresses physical, cognitive, and social skills and serves as a discharge site for physical, occupational, and speech therapies.

The driving force for the development of the Innovations program was the Medicare Part B capitation (Medicare B cap). As a result of the Balanced Budget Act of 1997 and the Skilled Nursing Facility Prospective Payment System (PPS), a monetary limit was established for physical, occupational, and speech therapy services to Medicare B beneficiaries. A $1500 per year cap was placed on occupational therapy services. A $1500 limit was also placed on physical and speech therapies combined, meaning that these two disciplines must split that $1500 benefit. Anyone working with these disciplines understands that $1500 does not provide a significant amount of service—1 or 2 weeks of treatment at most.

The Innovations program was designed to take over where physical, occupational, and speech therapy could no longer provide regular or frequent services. It served as a screening tool to determine whether skilled therapy interventions were needed or whether recreation therapy and restorative could increase function. When skilled therapy did provide service, Innovations was a discharge site where residents could maintain their newly acquired functional gains.

Since the development of Innovations, the Medicare B cap has been repealed. Yet, due to the large success and positive outcomes of this program, Innovations continues to serve residents, helping them to improve or maintain functioning. Therapists treating long-term care residents under

Medicare B now use Innovations as a group treatment setting, as well as a discharge site.

BENEFITS

In addition to assisting residents to maintain newly acquired functional gains, numerous other benefits exist for the Innovations program, including:

- Increased wheelchair mobility
- Increased ambulation
- Increased endurance
- Increased balance
- Increased strength
- Improved grip and fine motor skills
- Increased hand-eye coordination
- Improved visual tracking
- Increased flexibility
- Maintenance of current functional abilities
- Consistent use of compensatory strategies
- Increased initiation
- Increased motivation
- Increased social interaction
- Increased attention to task
- Improved nonverbal communication
- Improved social behavior
- Improved social communication
- Increased long-term memory
- Increased short-term memory
- Increased rapport with staff
- Increased involvement in the recreation therapy activity program
- Increased leisure skills
- Improved sequencing
- Improved ability to follow directions
- Improved word finding
- Improved problem solving
- Improved number and symbol matching

This list encompasses the basic benefits of a recreation therapy restorative program. Through regularly scheduled programs, lead by a trained and competent staff person, this program can achieve these benefits and more.

Using recreation and leisure to address physical and cognitive issues often distracts residents from their limitations, disabilities, or discomfort. "Activities that are normally pursued in leisure reflect certain characteristics that motivate participation while also producing desired affective and physical states" (Howe & Schwartzberg, 1995). In addition, using recreational and leisure interests disguises exercise, hiding potential discomfort and fatigue and thus enhancing the benefits to the individual. This is not a secret to recreation therapists who regularly use leisure to address functional issues. "Activity interventions in the physical, cognitive and psychosocial areas, along with leisure education, are collectively aimed at promoting optimal functioning, preventing further decline and rehabilitation of functional losses" (Howe & Schwartzberg, 1995).

Furthermore, groups are a natural component of life. "Groups are a part of people's experience not only in normal or healthy life but also in life interrupted by disease and distress (Howe & Schwartzberg, 1995). Life is lived in groups—families, school, places of employment, and social and religious organizations. Group interaction is normal. Groups are versatile, easily adaptable, and used to address a variety of goals. During groups residents motivate each other and provide encouragement. They also provide opportunities for socialization and relationship building. Finally, during groups residents can see that they are not alone—others experience the same struggles and limitations—creating a common bond and reducing the focus on oneself.

From a staff perspective, there are also a number of benefits. Improved teamwork and cooperation contributes to increased morale and job satisfaction. Group programs provide an opportunity to use time more effectively and efficiently. By gathering a group of individuals in one location, it reduces the amount of time staff must take to move from person to person throughout the building. It provides staff the chance to provide a therapeutic intervention in an effective and cost-efficient manner. "The group format shows clear signs of being both therapeutic and cost-effective" (Howe & Schwartzberg, 1995). Group work often lowers the cost of treatment. It provides two perspectives and observations of the same event. Every person views an experience differently. Staff are able to share their observations easily and gather input about various situations from different perspectives. Furthermore, groups provide more opportunities for creativity.

A cooperative program is extremely beneficial and accomplishes a variety of goals. "Rehab [and restorative] intervention often is achieved through a coordinated program of services that involves a team of professionals. Rehab intervention involves an activity program where the emphasis is on the development or reacquisition of skills" (Howe & Schwartzberg, 1995). Recreation therapy plays an important role in the restoration, maintenance, and improvement of functional abilities. Garner writes:

> Therapeutic recreation specialists have the responsibility for planning, organizing and directing recreation programs that have been medically approved . . . The content of each program is determined in consultation with other members of the treatment team . . . The primary purpose of the recreation therapist's work is to either restore a prior level of skill or develop new leisure skills and activity. This is important to the overall recovery process because the recreation therapist is able to help that patient attain not only a skill, but also a quality of life that is personally satisfying. (1994, p. xx)

PHASE 1: ASSESSMENT

Several tasks must be accomplished prior to implementation. This phase involves two types of assessments. First, the facility needed to be assessed. Second, the residents needed to be evaluated for inclusion in the Innovations program. In assessing the facility, ask the following questions:

- ☐ Does your facility have a need for such a program?
- ☐ Is an exercise program offered by your recreation therapy or restorative nursing staff? If yes, does it improve abilities or does it just give residents something to do?
- ☐ Is there a specific program to address cognitive issues and social skills? Is it therapeutic and outcomes focused?
- ☐ Do current programs maintain residents' functional abilities?
- ☐ Do residents get to the exercise, cognitive or social programs on a regular basis?
- ☐ Do disciplines work together to restore, maintain, or improve resident abilities?
- ☐ Is the current program effective in meeting physical, cognitive, and social needs?

Another facility consideration is the support of the management and leadership staff. The management team can make or break a program. The support and acceptance of certain key leadership staff will be needed. The administrator, director of nursing, therapy director, and restorative nurse are essential to the success of the program. Meet with each of these individuals to discuss the development of an Innovations program. Explaining the purpose of the program and its benefits and submitting a proposal for staffing, supplies, and room usage will clarify concerns and discuss the importance of this program. Providing this information demonstrates the value and cost effectiveness of recreation therapy.

Another issue related to the assessment of the facility is evaluating the resources available to carry out the program. Of utmost importance is the staff. Questions to ask include the following:

- ☐ Do you have a recreation therapist who can be responsible for the daily program?
- ☐ Is this person a team player?
- ☐ Does this person have strong leadership and organizational skills?
- ☐ Can this person interact with all members of the interdisciplinary team?
- ☐ Can he or she communicate the purpose of the program and work with other disciplines to ensure its success?
- ☐ Is he or she able to motivate residents?
- ☐ How are his or her clinical and documentation skills?
- ☐ Does he or she have a restorative/rehabilitation focus or background?
- ☐ Can other staff lead the program in this key person's absence?
- ☐ How is restorative nursing staffed? Will they be able to provide assistance?

Consider each of these questions before proceeding with program development. Without the right person facilitating and leading the program, Innovations will not succeed. Furthermore, it is important to have one person who is able to lead the program. "For consistency's sake, it's also important for the same therapist to lead the group at every session" (Weiler, 1998). Not only for consistency for the residents, but for consistency and accountability related to communication, documentation, organization, and overall operation of the program.

Financial resources are another consideration. Are there funds to hire a recreation therapist to head the Innovations program (if the facility does not have an RT on staff)? A recreation therapist has the educational background, skills, clinical experience, and focus for an Innovations program. To be truly therapeutic and achieve program goals, the right philosophy must drive service delivery. Furthermore, recreation therapists have educational training in group facilitation, leadership, activity analysis, and program development. They understand how to use various activities and tasks to work on functional skills related to different diseases and aging.

Also consider if the department or facility has funds to use for equipment purchases. Fortunately, this particular question is not as significant as the previous. With some creativity, the department can make its own equipment at little to no cost. Soda bottles filled with water make great 1-pound weights. Wooden dowels 12–18 inches long make excellent exercise equipment. A variety of word games, magazines, and newspapers are available for cognitive groups. A computer and questions are all one needs to create a memory book.

The final step in the assessment phase is evaluating the residents for inclusion in the Innovations program. After obtaining a complete list of the facility's long-term care residents, each individual must be considered for the program by asking these questions:

- ☐ Has this person had a recent functional (physical, cognitive, or social) decline? This does not mean they had a significant change enough to cause a status change on the minimum data set (MDS), although this may be the case.
- ☐ Is the resident functioning at their highest, most independent level? Could the resident realistically do more for themselves than they are at the present time? Consider dressing, grooming, hygiene, mobility, leisure involvement, eating, and socialization.
- ☐ Does this resident receive specialized restorative services? Are they on an ambulation or range of motion program? Do the certified nurse's aides (CNA) or restorative nursing staff provide one-to-one interventions to work on mobility or range of motion?
- ☐ Has this resident recently been discharged from physical, occupational, or speech therapies? Is so, what skills were being worked on with the resident? Why was the resident discharged? If it's because they refused, that's an issue that staff will need to be aware of. Is it due to meeting goals? Or to a lack of progress? A lack of progress with physical, occupational, or speech therapy does not mean the resident will not benefit from Innovations; however, it may mean the resident needs more time to progress than skilled therapy was able to provide.

To answer these questions, review the resident's medical chart and care plan and have discussions with staff. Consultation with the nursing unit coordinator provides valuable information. Discussions held with the CNAs, the restorative nursing staff, and the recreation therapy staff reveal additional information about specific residents that might benefit from the program. Social workers can also be consulted to find out what they see or hear from residents and their families.

After reviewing the resident list and gathering resident specific information, a decision can be made as to whether the facility has a need for an Innovations program. Implementation of an Innovations program might be considered if:

- 6–10 residents are identified as needing such a program
- Restorative nursing or recreation therapy staff have difficulty meeting the needs of residents to maintain their abilities
- There is limited staff in either department
- There is a need to reduce costs in restorative nursing or recreation therapy

Once the decision is made to have a program, the needs of the residents can be identified and decisions can be made as to what types of programs are to be developed and implemented. Programming ideas and activities will be selected based on their ability to contribute to program objectives and treatment goals (Peterson & Gunn, 1984). Furthermore, the number of residents needing Innovations services will be determined, which will also affect the staffing level and time commitment to the program.

PHASE 2: PLANNING

Once information has been gathered about which residents to include in the Innovations program, the planning can begin. This phase of development involves generating group ideas, completing activity analysis on the groups, developing goals, objectives, and criteria, educating staff, and gaining support. Planning and developing the program are time-consuming, but well worth the effort to create a quality restorative recreation therapy program.

The first step involves the program's design, including the *planning and selection of groups*. Recreation therapy can address physical, cognitive, social, leisure, emotional, and spiritual domains based on resident needs. After reviewing the residents' information, it should become obvious where programming needs to focus. Common areas to address are physical, cognitive, and communication issues using leisure tasks to address each of these domains. The following lists include a number of specific areas recreation therapy and the Innovations program can address.

Physical

- Upper extremity range of motion
- Lower extremity range of motion
- Fine motor skills
- Ambulation and mobility
- Balance
- Endurance
- Strength
- Coordination
- Visual tracking, scanning, and perception

Cognitive

- Long-term memory
- Short-term memory
- Following directions
- Attention to task
- Decision making
- Problem solving
- Sequencing
- Safety awareness
- Matching and identifying numbers or letters
- Math and reading skills

Communication

- Social skills
- Word finding
- Initiation
- Appropriate social behavior and interaction

Emotional

- Coping
- Adjustment

- Self-esteem
- Motivation
- Initiation
- Mood
- Behavioral issues

Leisure

- Adaptation of leisure interests
- Development of leisure skills and interests
- Leisure education and awareness
- Leisure involvement
- Quality of life issues

Once the focus areas are determined, group ideas can be brainstormed. What activities could be used to address these areas? Physical program ideas range from exercise to parachute games to balloon volleyball. Cognitive groups include reminiscing, word games, and current events. Communication can be addressed separately or through a cognitive group. **Appendix A** contains a more extensive list of group ideas.

From here, an *activity analysis* should be completed. "Activity analysis is the procedure of breaking down and examining the inherent characteristics of an activity" (Edginton, Hanson & Edginton, 1992). Through activity analysis, the various components of an activity are identified and analyzed, ranging from equipment needs to group setup to level of participation. The components are broken down to identify the functional abilities and skills needed for accomplishment. Despite the time it takes for completion, activity analysis is an extremely beneficial process. Greenblatt (1988) writes:

> An analysis of each individual element provides the program planner with a greater understanding of how the activity may help its client achieve successful participation This further enables the program planner to modify or adapt appropriate activities, which will allow for participation of the patient or client. (p. 57)

An activity analysis form should be completed for each possible activity or task used in one of the groups. A sample form is included in **Appendix B**.

The next significant step in the planning process is the *development of criteria*. Written criteria detail the specifics of the Innovations program. Identification of the objectives and goals of the program helps to keep the staff focused and establishes parameters and procedures for the program. Written entrance and exit criteria point out the conditions that must be met to be admitted or discharged from the program. This provides all staff with guidelines for which residents are appropriate for the program. It also gives the individual leading the Innovations program specific guidance for admitting and discharging residents based on their functional level, participation, and goals. The criterion also provides group ideas, length of the sessions, and frequency of the group to achieve its goals. Sample criteria for each group (physical, cognitive, and communication) are included in **Appendix C**. **Appendix D** provides a sample operational policy for the program.

When developing the criteria, review current policies and procedures of the recreation therapy, restorative nursing, and therapy departments. This provides guidelines for admission and discharge to the program. Most likely, such criteria will not be found in the recreation therapy policy book because long-term care has focused on providing activities to *all* residents to meet their leisure and recreational needs. Restorative nursing and therapy should both have policies that govern when they pick up and discharge a resident from their caseload. Criteria such as physical decline affecting functional abilities are common for admission to restorative or therapy caseloads. Criteria such as three consecutive refusals without a medical reason, meeting of established goals, or lack of progress are common reasons for discharge. Furthermore, the activity analysis for each group activity should be reviewed to determine what skills or adaptations are needed for involvement and participation in a particular activity. Completion of both of these tasks will reveal the criteria for admission and discharge from the Innovations program.

The next step in the planning phase is *education*. All staff must be educated about the purpose and process of the Innovations program. Everyone from CNAs to management staff must be aware of the program, the process for involving residents, and its benefits. Support from the administrator and management team will go a long way in encouraging support of all levels of staff. Furthermore, the management staff must be prepared to answer general questions of family members or staff and know where and to whom to direct questions.

Education of the housekeeping, maintenance, social work and dietary staff will prevent unnecessary interruptions. It will also help the program to run smoothly by having the room ready for groups. Furthermore, these departments will be able to adapt their schedule and work with the recreation therapy staff to meet resident needs. These departments can also be a referral source, such as social work noticing adjustment or coping problems, dietary noticing changes in fine motor abilities, and housekeeping observing problems in communication.

Educating the recreation therapy staff is also important. The RT staff must have a clear understanding of the program. They will be required to answer questions from other staff, residents, and families. They will also, on occasion, be required to lead the Innovations program in the absence of the recreation therapist. In addition, the RT staff will be an excellent resource for referrals since they interact with residents throughout the building and in different settings. The RT staff will be able to offer input into interventions that work with particular residents, to share information related to improvements or declines, and to follow through on a resident's plan of care after discharge from the Innovations program. Finally, the RT staff will be responsible for making adjustments in other programs and service to accommodate those not involved in the Innovations program.

Another key group requiring education will be the restorative nursing staff. The Innovations program should be developed closely with the restorative nurse. Often information does not filter down to the restorative aides doing the hands-on work. Cooperation with these staff members is critical to the success of the Innovations program. Restorative nursing staff must understand that Innovations is a compliment to their work, not a substitution or replacement. It is also important for them to realize that groups are a more efficient and effective way for them to complete their job tasks. Through this program, 10 or more residents can receive active and passive range of motion in one location simultaneously, thus requiring less intensive one-to-one interventions and assistance. Through groups, restorative nursing can reduce the hours required to perform one-to-one passive range of motion by bringing residents together in one location at the same time.

Finally, educating the CNAs and nurses is essential. Having support from this group will help the program run smoothly. With proper education and reminders, the staff will make sure residents are available and ready for groups. They will also be open to making suggestions or offering input into residents' current functional abilities and serve as a prime referral source. CNAs and nurses must understand the Innovations program to make appropriate referrals at the time declines or changes are observed. Educating CNAs and nurses should also reduce the number of interruptions by showing how important the program is and what its benefits are. This group will also observe the outcomes, gains, and improvements residents make during care and meal times. Furthermore, they will be the ones to get questions from families when recreation therapy staff are not available. **Appendix E** provides a sample for educating staff on the Innovations program.

The planning phase requires the most amount of time. Several of the key steps in this phase are demanding, repetitious, and time-consuming. However, developing program ideas, conducting activity analysis, establishing criteria, and educating staff will lead to the success of the Innovations program. "[After the] planning phase with careful consideration given to client needs, therapeutic goals, activity selection and program design, it is time to implement the plan" (Howe & Schwartzberg, 1995).

PHASE 3: IMPLEMENTATION

In the implementation phase several areas need to be addressed. These include staffing, scheduling, facilitation of groups, and managing the physical environment.

LEADERSHIP AND ROLES

The recreation therapist provides leadership for program and groups. The recreation therapist was chosen to lead the group due to leadership experience, therapeutic philosophy, and group facilitation training. As stated previously, it is important to have consistent staff and leadership to ensure effectiveness and continuity of Innovations.

The recreation therapist plans and organizes the group, determining with the restorative nurse which residents will be involved. The recreation therapist communicates to nursing staff and other disciplines which residents are involved and the program's schedule. The recreation therapist also serves as the primary facilitator of the groups. He or she selects the activity to be used in the group, provides instruction and leads the participants.

In this role as group leader, the recreation therapist creates a climate that provides support and encourages interaction. The RT selects an appropriate activity to work on identified goals, and adapts the activity to the needs and functional level of participants. "An activity is designed or selected to help members achieve [their identified] goal" (Cole, 1993). After gathering residents and starting the group, the RT provides verbal instruction and visual direction, while helping residents participate to their highest possible functioning.

With a group of 10–15 participants, it is difficult for the recreation therapist to provide individual hands-on assistance. The therapist must focus on involving all participants in the task at hand, which sometimes means limited individual interventions. For this reason the restorative aide is essential to the program.

The restorative aide serves an important complimentary role to the recreation therapist. The restorative aide helps gather residents for the group, walking as many of them as possible for therapeutic ambulation. During the exercise group, the restorative aide provides verbal cues and administers passive range of motion or passive resistance to residents while they are completing tasks. In cognitive groups, the restorative aide provides verbal cues and physical assistance to individual residents. They might also provide one-to-one interventions for a resident who is more cognitively impaired than other participants. Unlike the recreation therapist, the restorative aide is able to provide more individual interventions and hands-on assistance to residents to maximize their participation. The restorative aide assists the therapist in leading activities and provides encouragement to participants. The restorative aide also has the opportunity to lead groups if they are willing to do so.

Identification of roles and expectations of teamwork prior to implementation of groups is important. This makes responsibilities of each staff member clear and ensures completion of the group in a smooth and efficient manner. The process flows easier and communication can be aimed at participants, rather than at figuring out what is happening in the group.

Teamwork is important as recreation therapy and restorative nursing collaborate and work together to provide a quality program aimed at improving or maintaining functional abilities. Treatment goals are reached through the work of these two disciplines together; however, problems may arise.

> Effective teamwork is not easy. Conflicts arise when communication breaks down or when differences of opinions or interpretations of the patient's behavior are not resolved. Strong leadership, clarity of roles and responsibilities, and a willingness to devote time and effort to communication are essential [to effective teamwork].
> (U. S. Department of Health and Human Services, 1996)

SCHEDULE

Determining the schedule for the program will vary by facility. Consideration must be given to resident availability (ADLs, naps, visitors, meals, participation in recreational activities), staff availability (meetings, work schedules, responsibilities), the room availability (other uses—meals, meetings, visitation), and the daily schedule of the facility. After analyzing this information, one can determine a program schedule.

At the developing facility, the program runs Monday through Friday in the morning. Afternoons were considered, but due to the volume of visitors, limited availability of the room, naps, and the recreation program, mornings worked best. Exercise groups with the recreation therapist and restorative aide run from 9:45 a.m. to 10:15 a.m. It was found that nursing staff was able to complete ADLs, medication passes, and treatments prior to 9:45 for most residents so that the group could start without interruption.

Cognitive groups run from approximately 10:20 a.m. to 10:50 a.m., following exercise. Exercise gets the blood flowing and wakes participants up. Late morning for cognitive groups works well since residents are more alert and awake, therefore their cognitive abilities are sharper. Enough time is provided between groups to allow for the exchange of residents involved in the different groups. **Appendix F** displays a sample calendar of Innovations.

ENVIRONMENT

The environment is essential to the program's success and must be appropriate for the residents to participate. "Environment and procedures that are orderly and organized enhance the [participant's] ability to process information in an orderly and organized fashion. A cluttered or busy environment creates irrelevant, distracting stimuli in the . . . environment and impedes the [treatment] process" (Lewis & Bottomley, 1995).

Using a consistent room builds familiarity and comfort for participants and builds routine. Residents will recognize where they are going and for what purpose, as staff assist them to the Innovations room. The room should be in a centralized location if possible, since residents throughout the facility will be involved. It should be in a quiet area, with minimal distractions. Furniture should be able to be arranged to accommodate various activities.

As with any group activity, minimizing distractions is key to maintaining participants' attention and continued flow of the process. Signs can be hung on the room door noting that there is a group in session and should not be interrupted. Pointing this out during the education phase is important. All staff need to understand that interruptions distract participants and reduce the benefits of the group (particularly in cognitive groups). Medications and treatments should be administered before or after the group, never during. Visitors may attend the group with a resident, but are encouraged to sit as a passive observer.

The environment will have a significant impact on participation and the attention of residents. The environment should promote participation and social interaction. Participants should be encouraged to interact with each other, but should be considerate of the leader and the activity occurring. If residents feel safe and comfortable, they are more likely to participate. If they feel they are being monitored or mocked by other staff outside the room, participation will be negatively impacted. Providing a safe, comfortable, accepting environment will facilitate participation and thus, the attainment of goals.

GROUP STRUCTURE

In each group, the recreation therapist follows a routine or structure. Group begins with introductions—the therapist and restorative aide introduce themselves and clearly explain the activity. This sets the mood for the group and prepares participants for what is ahead. Participants are also encouraged to introduce themselves to help create a comfortable environment. Following this, the activity begins. Residents are encouraged to participate in all aspects of the task. If they are not able to complete the full task, they are encouraged to do what they can. Any movement is better than no movement. Upon completion of the activity, the RT seeks feedback from participants about the group and how the individuals are feeling. Prior to leaving, residents are given feedback and praised for their involvement. After residents return to their rooms, the recreation therapist and restorative aide talk about the group, complete their documentation and conduct an informal evaluation of the group.

It is important the group be planned ahead and well-organized; however, "groups should also stay flexible . . . Allowing patients to lead the group in directions they want to go can make group treatments worthwhile as well as fun" (Weiler, 1998).

Group size varies depending on the group and client needs. Exercise groups range from 8–15 participants. Typically exercise groups are approximately 10 residents working on strengthening, range of motion, endurance, and balance. Cognitive groups contain 4–8 residents. Focus areas for these participants include memory, attention, problem solving, and orientation. A restorative aide is present during both groups, providing individualized assistance and attention.

PARTICIPATION

Participation in the Innovations program varies daily for a number of reasons. Some of these are beyond the therapist's control; others can be controlled.

Resident participation is affected by how the individual feels—physically, mentally, and emotionally. Each individual's level of fatigue and arousal impacts their willingness and desire to participate. Feeling confused, depressed, or anxious also bears upon participation. Furthermore, the resident's interest in the activity and past experience with the task influence their participation. If the individual enjoyed bowling in the past, they are more likely to participate than if they had never done it.

Next, other staff affect participation. The timing of CNAs and nursing staff in getting residents ready for a group influences participation. Clients may arrive late to a group due to a number of factors. Arriving late, the individual might not fully comprehend what is occurring or might feel left out because they missed part of the group. Being hurried along in the morning may affect a person's mood and desire to participate. In addition, if the Innovations staff are not focused and talk among themselves, resident concentration and feelings of acceptance may be impacted.

While the therapist has no control over how an individual feels or what occurred earlier in the day, the recreation therapist can provide activities and tasks that are diverse, encourage active participation, and are of interest to participants. It is difficult to select a task daily that all participants will enjoy; therefore, variety allows residents to experience new activities, but also promotes participation in previous interests. Tasks that encourage active participation should be used to prevent boredom or sleeping during groups and to facilitate involvement.

In addition, "the willingness to be an active group participant and commitment to the treatment process will be strongly influenced by their understanding of what they can hope to gain from the treatment experiences offered" (Borg & Bruce, 1991). Therefore, it is important that the purpose of the group and task is explained to participants to increase their involvement. Helping residents understand the benefits of the task generates enthusiasm and goal accomplishment.

Another important component impacting participation is social interaction. "It has been said that people get as much out of a group activity as they put into it. When group members are interacting with one another, they are not only participating but also taking over some of the responsibility for the group. Interaction should be encouraged" (Cole, 1993). Social interaction automatically involves participants in an activity. Creative seating arrangements incorporate social interaction into group activities. Another intervention to encourage interaction is building reminiscing into different tasks and allowing residents to share their experiences and views.

Another influencing factor is the therapist. The therapist's attitude and excitement increases and generates enthusiasm among the participants. The therapist's skill at engaging residents and providing directions and cues also impacts participation.

Finally, environmental factors impact participation. The physical setup of the group, arrangement and comfort of furniture, noise level, and temperature of the room contribute to or distract from each individual's participation. The recreation therapist might not be able to directly control all of these environmental factors, but actions can be taken to minimize distractions.

DAY-TO-DAY OPERATIONS

Daily operation of the program varies based on staffing in all departments, room readiness, and resident availability. However, a typical routine can be established, as long as there is room for flexibility. **Appendix G** provides a sample of the day-to-day operations of Innovations.

DOCUMENTATION

As with all treatment, documentation is a major component of the program. "[The treatment] process involves an assessment of need, a statement of the problem, formulation of treatment goal(s), design of a treatment plan, implementation, monitoring and progress reporting, and designation of criteria for decision making regarding termination, continuation, or change" (Peterson & Gunn, 1984).

Assessing the need of the client is the first step in the process. As previously mentioned, a referral is made by a member of the interdisciplinary team or the recreation therapist notes a decline. An informal assessment occurs to determine if the resident meets the established program criteria. The recreation therapist consults with other staff members and reviews the medical chart to further evaluate the resident. If the resident meets program requirements, they are admitted to the program.

An "admission to Innovations" note is completed stating that the resident was referred and admitted into the program. The note explains the declines or changes, providing a brief description of the focus area(s) for the treatment plan. If a resident does not meet the criteria, this is noted in a progress note with a brief reason for the rejection. An acceptance note might look like this:

> *CTRS received referral for Innovations program from Nursing staff due to noted increased confusion and memory impairment. Upon review, CTRS also noted increased lethargy affecting the resident's ability to complete ADLs. Resident will be admitted to the Innovations program to address memory and attention 3 times per week for 4 weeks.*

Upon completion of the note, the recreation therapist develops the care plan. The care plan includes a problem, interventions, and a measurable goal. The developing facility uses a generic care plan problem to address all Innovations participants. The problem is which the developing facility uses on the care plan. Individualized interventions are noted, detailing what approaches will be used to achieve the established goal. Finally a measurable goal is written. A sample care plan for the resident mentioned in this example might be:

> *Problem*: Need for therapeutic interventions due to recent declines in cognition.
>
> *RT Interventions*:
>
> (1) Involve resident in Innovations cognitive group Monday through Friday at 10:15 a.m.
> (2) Provide verbal and visual cues to maintain attention.
> (3) Use resident's name to get attention.
> (4) Resident enjoys woodworking and music.
> (5) Provide hands-on task for resident to complete.
> (6) Praise involvement, participation, and remaining awake.
>
> *Nursing Interventions*:
>
> (1) Have resident ready for Innovations group Monday through Friday at 10:15 a.m.
> (2) Assist resident to Innovations room for group.
> (3) Provide verbal and visual cues for attention.
>
> *Restorative Interventions*:
>
> (1) Provide verbal and visual cues for attention to task.
> (2) Offer encouragement and praise.
> (3) Use resident's name to get attention.
>
> *Goal*: Resident will demonstrate increased attention to task as evidenced by remaining awake to actively complete a task with 1–2 verbal cues in a 30-minute Innovations group 3 times per week.
>
> *Goal Time*: One month

Additional care plan goals are mentioned in **Appendix H**.

A 1-month time frame is typically used for Innovations participants for several reasons. First, since many of these individuals are experiencing declines, changes in medical condition, and some type of mild cognitive impairment, one month allows time for interventions to take effect and provides an adequate time frame for improvements to occur. At times, improvements are noted quickly. Allowing a one-month time frame also provides time for carry-over into activities of daily living. Second, it allows the resident time to adjust to changes, to develop familiarity with the program and staff, and to feel comfortable, thus enhancing participation. Third, it often takes more time for the elderly to recover from changes in medical conditions.

Upon development of the care plan, the treatment plan is implemented. The resident's involvement in the program begins. Daily charting occurs, noting what activities the resident participated in, the person's level of participation (whether it was active or passive) and whether the individual's goal was met. At this facility, this is done in the daily recreation therapy charting done for all residents. For example:

Attended	*Innovations Cognitive Group*
Participation	*Active*
Goal met?	*Yes*

On a weekly basis, the recreation therapist reviews the care plan to ensure that it is current and appropriate. Modifications are made as needed. Then, the RT writes a weekly summary note describing the resident's participation, progress and attainment of goals in the past week. For example:

> *Resident actively participated in five Innovations cognitive groups during the week. Resident needed only one verbal cue for attention in each group. Resident fell asleep once during the week, but was easily awakened using identified interventions. Current goal to be continued one week to ensure carry-over to ADLs. CTRS will evaluate for further goals.*

If the resident continues to meet goals, new goals are written or more difficult issues are addressed. Once a resident reaches all goals or if they plateau and stop making gains, the resident is discharged from the Innovations program. Residents are also discharged from the program if:

- Skilled therapy picks the individual up to address the same issue
- Resident repeatedly refuses involvement (three times without medical reason)
- No improvements or changes are noted after four weeks of involvement
- Resident is socially inappropriate in group settings
- Resident declines due to an acute medical condition.

At the time of discharge, a discharge note is written summarizing the individual's participation and progress, and makes follow-up recommendations. This note might appear as follows:

> *Resident is being discharged from the Innovations program at this time. All goals have been successfully met and resident's attention is within functional limits. Upon admission, resident needed 5–7 verbal cues for attention to complete tasks. At this time, resident does not need verbal cues for attention related to task completion as evidenced by independent completion of ADLs. Resident actively participated in Innovations cognitive group five times a week for six weeks. It is recommended that resident continue to pursue mentally stimulating activities, such as reading in his room. Resident will be encouraged to attend cognitive group activities such as word games or trivia.*

Regular documentation is important to show the improvements and progress residents are making. Furthermore, documentation demonstrates the effectiveness and efficiency of the program to achieve significant outcomes. Finally, documentation assists in ensuring quality services that are achieving program goals.

COMMUNICATION

As with any program or service, communication is vital to the continuity and consistency of service. Several forms of communication have been implemented to communicate with staff about the Innovations program.

For the CNAs, residents involved in Innovations have a sign posted on their bathroom door reminding staff of the days and times the resident is involved in groups. These are hung at the time of admission to the program and removed when the resident is discharged (see **Appendix I**). A weekly notice is also provided to the CNA team, listing which residents from their hallway are scheduled for Innovations and the group times (see **Appendix J**). This weekly notice is also provided to the nursing supervisor, restorative nursing, therapy department, and recreation therapy staff. The notice informs all departments of which residents are involved in the program, including the groups and times the resident is occupied. Finally, information on Innovations involvement is included on each resident's care sheet, which is used for the daily provision of care.

To communicate with the nurses, a weekly memo is sent to the nursing coordinator on each hallway. This memo asks the nursing staff for referrals and information on those who have changes or declines. It also includes the names of residents recently admitted to the program (see **Appendix K**).

Written reminders are used in various ways to provide information about resident involvement in Innovations. Verbal communication is just as important. The recreation therapist contacts nurses weekly to ensure that referrals are made and to communicate participants' progress. The RT also has contact with the restorative nurse on a weekly basis to discuss issues and participants.

Furthermore, regular verbal reminders of the program are provided daily. The recreation therapist will remind CNAs that a resident is in Innovations and the location of the group for transportation reasons. While the recreation therapist does not want to nag, often residents are taken to the wrong location or do not get to the group because of oversight. Verbal communication must be handled delicately to prevent friction and irritation related to the reminders.

PHASE 4: EVALUATION

Measuring the outcomes of a restorative recreation program is an essential function of the program. Evaluation helps to determine if the program should continue and what (if any) modifications should be made.

> Evaluation as it relates to assessment and intervention will focus on a careful appraisal of client needs, treatment goals and objectives, progress measurement and the overall efficacy of the intervention in terms of bringing about the targeted behavior specified in the individual treatment plan and in the overall program goals and objectives. (Howe, 1995, p. 141)

There are several ways to evaluate the program and each programmer may wish to focus on different aspects. Evaluation of the program's benefits can be done daily, weekly, monthly, and quarterly.

DAILY EVALUATION

Daily evaluation should occur for two aspects of the program: group participation and performance. The therapist should evaluate the client's level of participation daily. Questions to consider include:

- ☐ Did the resident participate actively or passively?
- ☐ Did he or she need cues and if so, to what extent?
- ☐ Did he or she have limited participation due to complaints of pain or fatigue? Should these complaints be addressed by nursing?
- ☐ Did the pace of the group move along too quickly or slowly for the individual? Was he or she unable to keep up?
- ☐ What can the therapist do differently tomorrow to ensure this does not happen again?

- ☐ What might help the individual have greater success next time?

This type of evaluation can be performed informally by the therapist, using either a mental checklist or a short written list.

A simple breakdown of the day's events can point out what strengths and weaknesses were exhibited by both participants and the program. If an issue arises in the actual facilitation or implementation of the group, the therapist can attempt to correct it for the next group. However, if the issue relates to a client's personal participation, this needs to be reflected in the care plan and progress note. It is also important to evaluate group participation on a daily basis to help ensure any problematic issues are dealt with promptly and appropriately.

Daily evaluation of the client's progress is also important. This can be done in various formats, whether through a progress note daily or a note in the chart stating whether his or her goal was met. Documenting goals met is useful in reviewing the client's care plan. By knowing how often the client's goal was achieved, the therapist will have a better idea of whether or not the goal should be continued, altered, or discontinued. It also helps to determine if the client is appropriate for the program or should be discharged.

WEEKLY EVALUATION

Weekly evaluation is also an important component of the overall evaluation process. Three areas that can be considered weekly include outcomes, goals, and the individuals involved in the program. The therapist evaluates the outcomes of the program weekly to ensure that the focus is on the precise needs of the residents. For example, if after evaluating the week's programming the therapist finds that sequencing was addressed three times for a group without problems in sequencing, adjustments must be made. To achieve the desired outcomes, the appropriate interventions must be used. Weekly evaluation of observed outcomes enables the therapist to determine if changes are needed in programming, setup or facilitation of the group.

Closely related to outcomes are the goals of each participant. A weekly evaluation of the progress (or lack thereof) should be completed, considering the following questions:

- ☐ Is the client consistently meeting his/her goal independently?
- ☐ Is he or she doing so only with cues?
- ☐ How many times a week is the goal being met?
- ☐ What difficulties has the client experienced during the week?

- ☐ What can the therapist do differently to help the client?
- ☐ Is the client not meeting his or her goal because they are not consistently in group?
- ☐ Is he or she refusing or are the CNAs not getting the client ready on time?

In addition, a weekly evaluation of the program should include consideration of the residents involved. Is each client still appropriate? Are there other clients that should be added to the group? This is a good opportunity to determine if clients should continue with the program or be discharged.

Weekly contact with nursing is important to determine if there are other residents displaying declines who may benefit from a restorative recreation therapy program. It is also an ideal time to touch base with the restorative nurse to see if there are residents who have shown declines in range of motion. The therapist can also check to see if there are Medicare A patients with a discharge plan of long-term care being discharged from skilled therapy. Weekly evaluation of the participants will lead to a more varied and diversified group, as well as ensure that the appropriate people are involved in the program.

MONTHLY EVALUATION

Monthly evaluations are done in several ways. Quality improvement audits should be conducted to evaluate the types of groups provided. This demonstrates if there is sufficient variety in programming, how many participants were served, how many groups were provided, and what problems were significant.

Care plans should also be evaluated monthly. The therapist should reevaluate care plans after looking over the client's participation and progress for the month. If the client has been consistently meeting his or her goals, the therapist should determine if further participation can be beneficial or if no further progress can be made. If the resident is not meeting goals consistently, should the goal be changed or should the client be discharged? The client may need different interventions for successful participation. Monthly evaluation is an ideal time to analyze the client's carc plan. The therapist can look over the weekly notes of the client's participation and outcomes and use this information as a key to determining the next step for the client.

QUARTERLY EVALUATIONS

Quarterly evaluations may be done as part of the facility's quality improvement program. **Appendix L** provides a sample audit to review the effectiveness, quality, and variety of the program. Monitoring the facility's Quality Indicator report and MDS for residents noted with a decline in range of motion is another evaluation. (The Quality Indicator report compiles data from the MDS to identify issues related to quality of care.) Feedback should also be sought from individuals involved in the daily operation of the program to identify areas for improvement. **Appendix M** provides a sample evaluation form.

Furthermore, an informal evaluation of the daily operations of the program should also be performed on a regular basis. Questions to ask include: Would starting 15 minutes later increase participation? Do the CNAs truly understand their role? Are other disciplines making appropriate referrals?

Regular and consistent evaluations can be frustrating if negative aspects are found. However, the sooner issues are identified, the quicker they can be corrected. Constantly changing and improving the program will make it stronger. While evaluation of the program is a lengthy process, it should be done on a regular basis to ensure a successful program.

INNOVATIONS WITHIN OTHER PROGRAMS

This restorative recreation therapy program can be undertaken within other programs, such as an activity or restorative program. Although it is recommended that a certified therapeutic recreation specialist (CTRS) run the program, this is not practical for many facilities. A CTRS has the training and education to implement an effective restorative program, as well as the skills to evaluate and assess client functioning and outcomes. However, others can be trained to facilitate the Innovations program under the direction of a CTRS. If a facility is unable to have a CTRS run the program, the Innovations program can be placed within the activity or restorative nursing program.

WITHIN AN ACTIVITY PROGRAM

Within an activity program, the responsibilities of the CTRS would be indirect, rather than direct facilitation of the program. The recreation therapist would receive the referral and complete an assessment to determine if placement is appropriate. They would establish the specific guidelines for the program. It would be the recreation therapist's responsibility to monitor and evaluate outcomes, including range of motion assessments, writing progress notes, and developing care plans. The recreation therapist, in conjunction with the staff member running the program, should make the decision to continue or discharge a resident from the program. Furthermore, the recreation therapist and activity assistant would discuss intervention and group ideas to ensure that the appropriate outcomes will be attained. Responsibilities of the activity assistant would be to lead the group, as well as chart daily participation and achievement of goals each day.

The activity assistant should receive specialized training to have a better understanding of the program and recreation therapy interventions for each resident. First, there should be training to help the assistant understand the program philosophy, in particular the therapeutic value of activity, as well as the functional focus of Innovations. Training should include the basics of documentation. The assistant must have knowledge and basic understanding of the various components and mechanisms of documentation. If a recreation therapist is unable to provide documentation support, the assistant will require specialized training in care planning. Measurable, individualized, and functional goal writing should be emphasized. Furthermore, training should focus on activity analysis, understanding how to breakdown activities into their various components to understand the goals, skills required, and outcomes of involvement. And finally, training should cover range of motion assessments, administration of passive range of motion, ambulation, and transfers.

If restorative nursing can be involved in the program, this should be encouraged. Having extra assistance in exercise and cognitive groups allows residents to receive more individualized attention and assistance. Furthermore, having an additional person in the group provides the opportunity for involvement by more participants.

WITHIN A RESTORATIVE NURSING PROGRAM

The Innovations program within a restorative nursing program should be supervised by a restorative nurse, as required under long-term care regulations. Restorative aides will need the same training as the activity assistant, including the philosophy of the program. Restorative staff should already have extensive training in range of motion assessments, passive range of motion, ambulation, and transfers.

Restorative aides will require special training in group dynamics, leadership, and facilitation of activities. They will need to understand how various individuals and groups influence participation and involvement. Activity analysis should be emphasized as well so that appropriate interventions can be selected to accomplish goals. Restorative aides will need to acquire equipment and resources to utilize for exercise and cognitive groups, some of which might be shared with the activity program.

In addition to leading the group, restorative aides should complete the daily documentation of participation and goal attainment. The recreation therapist or restorative nurse should provide supervision and consultation on group ideas and interventions, documentation, and outcomes.

OTHER CONSIDERATIONS

Two additional considerations for the Innovations program are Medicare A patients and cotreatments.

If the facility has a Medicare A program, consideration should be given to Innovations in conjunction with the Medicare A program. When will referrals take place? Before or after therapy intervention? Who will see the patient first and then decide about the program? Based on experience, it is recommended that a patient be referred to Innovations after discharge from all therapies to ensure that the patient is available for group and therapy sessions. Conflicts arise when therapists want to treat the same patient at the same time. Once ready to discharge the patient, the therapist refers to the recreation therapist and includes Innovations in the discharge plan.

This facility found that Innovations is an excellent transition tool for patients who have come into the facility for rehabilitation on Medicare A, but who will be staying long-term care. In addition to addressing the improvements or maintenance of functional abilities, Innovations enables a patient to transition to long-term care, easing the fear or awkwardness of moving into a nursing home. It provides an opportunity for patients to begin developing relationships and rapport with other long-term care residents and staff.

For Medicare A patients involved in Innovations, minutes can be included in Section T of the Minimum Data Set. Section T1, entitled *Special Treatments and Procedures*. This allows a CTRS to record the minutes and frequency of treatment to demonstrate the importance and use of recreation therapy within skilled nursing facilities. Specific criteria must be met to complete Section T1a. These criteria include the following:

- Treatment must be provided in 15-minute increments
- Treatment must be physician ordered, including indication of the frequency, duration, and scope of treatment (see **Appendix N**)

- Treatment must go beyond the general activity program offered by the facility

Treatment services, aimed at improving functional abilities, must be provided by a therapeutic recreation specialist or by a therapeutic recreation assistant whose work is directed by the CTRS In these cases, Section T1a should be used for Medicare A patients involved in Innovations.

A final consideration is the use of Innovations for cotreatments with occupational, physical, and speech therapies for Medicare B patients. Under the Balanced Budget Act of 1997, PPS regulations permit therapists to treat at a ratio of one therapist to four patients. Group treatment is encouraged under this new system. Therefore, consideration must be given to how these group treatments will work. Who will run the group? How many residents will be allowed into the group? What will roles for each therapist be? This facility allows Innovations to be used for cotreatments for Medicare B patients. (There is a separate program for Medicare A group treatments.) Speech therapy is the discipline that most often uses these groups to address the cognitive functioning of long-term care residents.

CASE STUDIES

This section presents two residents involved in the program to demonstrate the various benefits and improvements noted through involvement in the Innovations program. These two case studies demonstrate the excellent outcomes and benefits of the physical and cognitive programming of Innovations.

CASE STUDY 1: JAMES

BACKGROUND

James is an 83-year-old male admitted 15 months ago after suffering a right-side stroke, resulting in left neglect. James was on skilled therapy, using his 100 Medicare A days. He was discharged from therapy due to lack of progress in occupational, physical, and speech therapy.

FUNCTIONING PRIOR TO INTERVENTION

Physical. James' stroke affected his left extremities—his left upper extremity was flaccid and his left lower extremity had limited movement. His right upper and lower extremities were fully functional. James stood and ambulated with a platform walker and maximum assistance of two people.

He was able to transfer with maximum assistance of two people. James had poor trunk control and a tendency to lean to the left. James was unable to toilet or dress himself independently. James also demonstrated visual neglect on his left side. He was independent with wheelchair mobility.

Cognitive. James' cognitive deficits were also impaired. Although James presented as cognitively high functioning in social situations, in further conversing with him, his deficits became apparent. His attention to task was poor and he needed moderate to maximum cues for task completion. When asked to complete a task, he would not make eye contact and would fiddle with objects as opposed to initiating tasks.

Problem solving was one of his most significant deficits. James was unable to identify safety hazards—running into objects rather than negotiating his wheelchair around them safely. He yelled out, "nurse, nurse" repeatedly rather than using his call light. He had difficulty with pragmatics related to impulsivity. James was unrealistic about his deficits, believing that "someday" he would improve and return home.

James had poor recall and processing. He was unable to recall what happened earlier in the day. Short-term memory and orientation to time were impaired. He had difficulty processing information as evidenced by his inability to stop an action he has been told three times in five minutes not to do. He had difficulty making decisions independently, requiring moderate to maximum cues.

Communication. James' verbal responses were limited. Although he did not lose his ability to communicate verbally, he lost his desire to do so. James responded with head nods or hand signals. James needed moderate to maximum encouragement, extra time to verbally respond and make eye contact.

Emotional. James' emotional state was also affected by his stroke. He was depressed and socially withdrawn. James did not initiate social interactions with others, despite being a very social person prior to his stroke. He needed moderate to maximum cues to respond when others interacted with him. Although James' wife visited regularly, his mood did not improve when she was present. He was tearful at times and demonstrated a flat affect. James had great difficulty coping with and adjusting to his losses. He stated feeling worthless and lonely.

INTERVENTION PLAN

James' Innovations treatment plan was to exercise five times a week to address range of motion, strengthening, and trunk control. James was transferred into an armless chair to improve trunk control and a weight was added to his left lower extremity to address strengthening. Staff encouraged wheelchair mobility with left lower extremity. James was also involved in a cognitive group five times a week to address his many cognitive issues. Although James' emotional issues were not formally addressed in a structured group, staff attempted to address these issues (particularly social interaction) during these groups.

Recreation therapy interventions included encouraging eye contact, establishing positive and therapeutic rapport, and encouraging verbal responses at all times. James was also seated next to sociable men who had similar interests and personalities.

FUNCTION AFTER INTERVENTION

During the first six months of his participation in Innovations, James showed dramatic improvements. He began communicating verbally with the recreation therapist. His initiation improved, and he began to interact more with others. Physically, he acquired some return in his left leg, though it was limited. He was using a 2-pound weight on his leg to continue to build strength.

Upon gaining return to his left lower extremity, James' affect greatly improved. He verbalized and smiled more often. James was also reevaluated and seen by physical therapy to address ambulation, balance, and transfers. While James' gait improved with increased movement, it still was not functional, requiring moderate to maximum assist of one staff member. Physical therapy explored the use of a merry walker, a device that encompasses an individual allowing them to walk within the frame, and includes a seat and bars for standing, ambulating or transferring from sit to stand. This was James' request, but the attempt was unsuccessful. After a short time of physical therapy, James plateaued and was again discontinued from therapy.

In the next few months, James began to decline slightly. He appeared more withdrawn, depressed, and lethargic. He began to develop difficulties in grip release with his right hand. James' antidepressant medication was increased without apparent success in mood improvement. After approximately one year of involvement in the Innovations program, James left the facility to attend an inpatient rehabilitation program at the request of his family. James returned appropriately one week later with the same physical and cognitive abilities he had left with; however, his emotional state had greatly declined due to the unsuccessful rehabilitation attempt.

CURRENT SITUATION

James was readmitted to the Innovations program where his treatment plan is now to maintain his current functional abilities. He continues to be withdrawn and has increased lethargy. Aside from the Innovations program, James is now participating in and initiating volunteer work on a daily basis within the facility. James has stated he enjoys this and it makes him feel purposeful. James' verbal communication is still limited, however he is able to talk openly about his deficits and his emotions with the recreation therapist who leads Innovations. He has developed a positive relationship with her in which she is able to encourage him to verbally express himself to others. James is involved in the long-term care recreation therapy program daily and enjoys going outdoors in his wheelchair with his wife. At this time, James is working on ambulating with physical therapy using a hemicane with contact guard assistance.

Innovations has helped James improve in several ways. The relationship that was formed between James and the recreation therapist was an unexpected benefit, as was the improvement that volunteering has brought to him.

CASE STUDY 2: ELAINE

BACKGROUND

Elaine is an 84-year-old female with a primary diagnosis of left-side stroke with right neglect, and a secondary diagnosis of Parkinson's Disease. Elaine was admitted to the facility for long-term care from another nursing home. She was admitted 3 years after her stroke. Elaine worked with occupational and physical therapy, and upon discharge from therapy was admitted to the Innovations program to continue addressing range of motion and strengthening.

FUNCTIONING PRIOR TO INTERVENTION

Physical. Elaine was unable to bear weight and thus used a wheelchair. Her transfers required the use of a mechanical lift. She had limited nonfunctional use of her right upper and lower extremities. Elaine's right leg was approximately four inches shorter than her left, causing her to wear a built-up shoe. She was able to propel her wheelchair independently, using her left side; however, Elaine complained of difficulty with propelling her wheelchair and needed encouragement to do so. Elaine's grip in her left hand was weak; therefore, she used built up utensils for eating.

Cognitive. Elaine had no cognitive issues upon admission to the facility. She scored 22 out of 22 on a cognitive test used at the facility.

Communication. Elaine had no difficulty communicating.

Emotional. Elaine showed minimal signs and symptoms of depression. She adjusted quickly to placement but continued to complain about not being about to ambulate. Elaine believed that the therapists at both facilities did not do enough to help her walk again. She was unrealistic in her hopes of walking or gaining functional use of her right side.

Social. Elaine enjoyed interacting with others and was a social person. At times, she was impatient with others who were confused. She had difficulty understanding that others were more impaired than she was.

INTERVENTION PLAN

Elaine was referred to Innovations to address her range of motion in her right side and for wheelchair mobility. The recreation therapist also addressed strengthening in her right leg. Elaine participated in the exercise group five times a week for 30 minutes each day. Due to weakness in her right leg and the thickness of her shoe sole, her shoe was removed during group. This enabled Elaine to flex her right leg without catching her foot on the carpet. After Elaine was able to do this, the recreation therapist began using a 2-pound weight on her right leg.

FUNCTION AFTER INTERVENTION

Upon completion of a range of motion assessment, Elaine gained 15 degrees of range of motion in her left arm in both flexion and extension, and 10 degrees in adduction and abduction. She increased her right arm flexion and extension by 40 degrees, and 70 degrees in adduction and abduction. Her left leg became stronger as evidenced by being able to flex her leg with the built-up shoe on. Due to Elaine's significant improvements, she was discharged from Innovations.

Elaine had a difficult time adjusting from Innovations groups to participating in the large group program. She felt that she was being "kicked out" and wondered why she could not continue participating in Innovations. She also had difficulty seeing the progress she had made as important, and instead focused on why she could not walk or functionally use her right side.

CURRENT SITUATION

Elaine was referred to the Innovations program five months after being discharged from the program due to decreased range of motion in her right upper extremity. She is again making progress; however, she continues to feel that she should be able to walk and use her right side functionally.

CONCLUSION

Innovations is an excellent program that addresses the physical, cognitive, communication, emotional, and social needs of long-term care residents while improving or maintaining their functional abilities. Innovations integrates recreation therapy and restorative nursing to make a significant improvement in the residents' lives.

Some outcomes are obvious, such as improvements in range of motion or increased strength, but numerous unexpected results also occur. These benefits are often not apparent at the time of treatment but become obvious in daily living outside the Innovations program. Many of these benefits, such as increased socialization or rapport with others, are difficult to quantify but can be observed in the resident's daily interactions with staff or family or involvement in recreation programs.

Using recreation and leisure to improve quality of life and address physical and cognitive issues has been proven beneficial in the literature and within the field of recreation therapy. Recreation and leisure distracts residents from their limitations, disabilities, or discomfort while working to make functional improvements. Furthermore, the use of group treatments has also been proven effective for improving or maintaining functional abilities. Groups are a natural part of life and an effective treatment modality for therapists. Groups are a cost-effective, efficient, natural setting for an Innovations program.

While the process of program development is intensive, the program makes a significant contribution. Assessment, planning, implementation, and ongoing evaluation create a program of great value. Innovations improves functional abilities and enhances psychosocial aspects of life. Maintaining dignity and independence while improving physical, cognitive, and psychosocial functioning are worthy goals of any program. Costs are typically minimal, and creativity and activity analysis can create many beneficial and therapeutic tasks that enhance the program. Furthermore, with a focus on teamwork, Innovations brings multiple disciplines together to improve the lives of residents. Innovations makes a difference.

APPENDIX A

GROUP ACTIVITY IDEAS

Cognitive

Board games
- Life Stories
- Monopoly
- Sequence
- Sorry
- Scrabble

Card games
- Uno (simplify by using only numbered cards and match color or number)
- Skipbo
- Crazy Eights
- Kings in the Corner
- Go Fish
- Penny Ante

Table games
- Yahtzee (simplify by only doing top portion of score card)
- Boggle
- Dominoes
- Bingo
- Scattergories
- Taboo
- Outburst

Cooking

Reminiscing
- Life History—develop a series of questions about personal experiences (e.g., Where were you born? What are your children's names?) and write out memories
- Read excerpts from books or magazines to spark memories

Current events
- Use newspapers, magazines, TV news programs (e.g., C-Span, CNN)

Problem-solving scenarios (e.g., What would you do if...?)

Orientation games

Proverbs (e.g., Finish this statement: An apple a day...)

Sentence completion
Story reading

- Ask questions for recall of information (e.g., What happened in this story? Who was the main character in this story?)
- Make up story or use printed material

Hangman

Physical

Upper extremity exercises

- Dowels
- Weights
- Plates: use hard plastic plates for upper extremity range of motion
- Specific upper extremity exercises only working arm, shoulders, neck, and face muscles (e.g., shoulder rolls, bicep curls)

Lower extremity exercises

- Kickball
- Soccer—set sides/positions and shot for goal
- Specific lower extremity exercises working only leg, back, and trunk muscles (e.g., leg extensions, ankle rotations)

Active games

- Lawn dice
- Bocce
- Dice exercise—develop cards with different exercises written on them and have participants draw a card and roll the dice; participants perform the activity on the card, doing the number of repetitions indicated by the dice
- Hokey pokey
- Chicken dance
- Parachute games
- Theme exercises—select a theme and do movements associated with theme, such as exercises associated with spring cleaning (e.g., washing windows, shaking rugs), sports (e.g., pitching a baseball), or winter activities (e.g., shoveling, decorating a Christmas tree)
- Charades
- Penny pitch—create target game and toss pennies to gain points
- Basketball—shoot ball into hoop or laundry basket
- Balloon volleyball
- Bowling

APPENDIX B

ACTIVITY ANALYSIS: MASTER COPY

Group Title ____

Group Size Small (<12) ____ Large (>12) ____ One-to-One ____

Time Required _______________ Room ___________________________

Equipment Needed ____

Frequency ______________ Staff to Patient Ratio_________________

Skills Required

Physical ____

____

Cognitive ____

____

Social/Communication ____

____

Sensory ____

____

Emotional ____

____

Leisure____

____

Goals and Objectives

Physical ______________________________

____

Cognitive______________________________

____

Social/Communication______________________________

____

Sensory ______________________________

____

Emotional ______________________________

____

Leisure______________________________

____

Adaptations

____

____

____

____

____

ACTIVITY ANALYSIS: EXAMPLE

Group Title *Bingo*
Group Size Small (<12) ____ Large (>12) *X* One-to-One ____

Time Required *45-60 minutes* Room *Recreation room*

Equipment Needed *Bingo cards, chips, tracking page, microphone*

Frequency *One time per week* Staff to Patient Ratio *1:40*

Skills Required

Physical *arm extension and flexion, crossing midline, fine motor grip, trunk and head control, hand-eye coordination, gross motor control*

Cognitive *recall, number and letter recognition, reading ability, following directions, processing, attention to task, initiation*

Social/Communication *verbal expression, pragmatics, self-control*

Sensory *auditory comprehension, visual scanning, visual tracking, tactile, auditory, and visual discrimination*

Emotional *self-control, socially appropriate behavior, ability to cope with losing*

Leisure *no specific leisure skills required*

Goals and Objectives

Physical *grasp objects, maintain sitting position, demonstrate control of upper extremity and fine motor movements*

Cognitive *maintain attention to task, recognize numbers and letters, follow directions, recall information, initiate and complete task*

Social/Communication *express self, display self-control, demonstrate appropriate social behavior*

Sensory *distinguish numbers and letters, visually scan and track for proper placement of chip, distinguish when gripping chip, distinguish visual and auditory stimuli*

Emotional *appropriate self-expression, decreased anxiety in group, expression of enjoyment, no s/s of depression*
Leisure *pursuit of previously enjoyed activity or learning a new skill*

Adaptations

Larger chips for fine motor impairments, signs for numbers called or hand signals for bingo for auditory impairments, picture or color bingo for cognitive impairments, large print cards for visual impairments, upright card and post-it markers for gross motor impairments.

APPENDIX C

INNOVATIONS CRITERIA

Cognitive Program
Groups are held for 30 minutes, up to 5 times per week

Objectives

- Improve problem solving ability
- Increase attention to task
- Improve short-term memory
- Improve long-term memory
- Improve recall of information
- Increase safety awareness
- Enhance new learning
- Increase social interaction
- Improve sequencing skills
- Improve orientation
- Improve ability to follow directions

Entrance Criteria
One or more of the following must be met

- Appropriate referral
- Appropriate social behavior for group setting
- Recent decline in cognitive abilities
- Potential to have improvement in cognitive functioning as determined by recreation therapist or restorative nurse
- Deficits in cognitive abilities

Exit Criteria
One or more of the following must be met

- Resident has met goal(s)
- Resident showed no signs of improvement after four weeks
- Resident is not socially appropriate in group situations
- Resident shows cognitive decline related changing medical condition
- Resident refused group three times
- Skilled therapy is providing interventions

Physical Program

Groups are held for 30 minutes, up to 5 times per week

Objectives

- Increase endurance
- Improve range of motion
- Increase strength
- Increase gross motor functioning
- Increase fine motor abilities
- Improve wheelchair mobility or ambulation
- Maintain functional abilities

Entrance Criteria

One or more of the following must be met

- Appropriate referral
- Appropriate social behavior for group setting
- Decreased range of motion
- Decline in endurance
- Decreased strength
- Decreased gross or fine motor ability
- Other change in physical functioning
- Potential to improve in physical functioning, as determined by the recreation therapist or restorative nurse

Exit Criteria

One or more of the following must be met

- Resident has met goal(s)
- Resident showed no signs of improvement after four weeks
- Resident is not socially appropriate in group situations
- Resident shows physical decline related to changing medical condition
- Resident refused group three times
- Skilled therapy is providing interventions

Communication Program

Groups are held for 30 minutes, up to 5 times per week

Objectives

- Increase social skills
- Improve communication
- Increase long-term memory
- Increase short-term memory
- Improve attention to task
- Improve word finding abilities

Entrance Criteria

One or more of the following must be met

- Appropriate referral
- Appropriate social behavior for group setting
- Decline or difficulty in any of the objective areas
- Decline in communication skills
- Decreased social interaction
- Potential to have improvement in cognitive functioning as determined by recreation therapist or restorative nurse

Exit Criteria

One or more of the following must be met

- Resident has met goal(s)
- Resident showed no signs of improvement after four weeks
- Resident is not socially appropriate in group situations
- Resident shows physical decline related to changing medical condition
- Resident refused group three times
- Skilled therapy is providing interventions

APPENDIX D

OPERATIONAL POLICIES AND PROCEDURES

Policy Statement

Small group activities will be provided for residents who have shown a decline in functional abilities or need specialized interventions for maintaining their function. The purpose of these groups is to improve and/or maintain functional abilities and skills using recreation, as well as to continue normal activity and assist residents in maintaining their highest possible functional level for the greatest amount of time.

Policy Interpretation and Implementation

1. The recreation therapist is responsible for overseeing the planning and implementation of restorative small group activities.
2. The recreation therapist and restorative nurse will discuss (on a regular basis) which residents have declined and if they are appropriate for Innovations. A resident must meet certain criteria to be admitted to the Innovations program.
3. Other staff (e.g., nurses, therapists) can make a referral for involvement in Innovations when a decline in physical, cognitive, or communication skills is noted. The recreation therapist will check with the nursing unit supervisors weekly to discuss potential residents for inclusion in the program.
4. The recreation therapist will review the referral and share this information with the restorative nurse. A decision will be made by the recreation therapist as to which groups the resident should be involved in based on the criteria, as well as the resident's needs and goals.
5. A variety of groups and activities are used to restore functional abilities.
6. Therapists (occupational, physical, speech) are encouraged to attend small group activities with their Medicare Part B residents to work on functional goals and skills. Therapists may refer residents to these groups as a screening method to determine if a resident needs skilled therapy interventions, or as a discharge plan to follow up on goals already met.
7. Attendance and participation will be charted by the recreation therapist on departmental forms. Additional notes related to functional skills and abilities will be noted in the recreation therapy progress note.

8. A resident's progress (or lack of progress) toward established goals will be reviewed monthly. At this time, a decision will be made to determine whether the resident should continue with the program. A resident must continue to meet the criteria or be working toward specific goals to remain in Innovations.
9. At the time of discharge, a note will be written reviewing the resident's involvement and progress.
10. Each Friday, a schedule for the Innovations program will be given to each hallway, detailing which residents are involved in the groups for the coming week. The recreation therapist will make known any changes at least one day prior. Appropriate staff will be notified of these changes.
11. An Innovations book is kept in the recreation therapy office and contains the program's forms, policies, group admission and discharge criteria, and other relevant information.

APPENDIX E

INNOVATIONS EDUCATION

Management Staff

Presented by Recreation Therapy Director

- Present overview of Innovations program, including who will run it, how it will run, why it is being implemented, and where it will occur.
- Discuss the role of other departments, including the importance of nursing and housekeeping in daily operations and the roles of social work and therapy.
- Answer questions about the impact on residents not involved and how it will affect other departments. Present plan for inclusion of these residents into general recreation program instead of small group program previously offered.

Recreation Therapy Staff

Presented by Recreation Therapist and Recreation Therapy Director

- Provide overview of Innovations program, including its purpose, selection of residents, participants, and reasons for new program. Discuss how this is a part of a recreation therapy program and demonstrate how it accomplishes the department mission.
- Discuss what changes are being seen in the resident population, changes in demand for therapy, modifications in regulations, or expectations, such as increased attention to loss of range of motion.
- Present overview of quality indicators (e.g., decline in range of motion and ADLs). Explain how recreation therapy can improve these areas through the program and thus enhance each resident's quality of life.
- Emphasize that residents previously in small groups must be incorporated into large groups during Innovations time. Provide suggestions for interventions and adaptation for more impaired residents.
- Provide training on how to lead Innovations groups. Schedule time for each staff member to assist or observe operation of Innovations program.
- Answer questions about the impact on residents not involved and how it will affect other departments. Present plan for inclusion of these residents into general recreation program instead of small group program previously offered.

Restorative Aides

Presented by Recreation Therapist with Restorative Nurse

- Discuss the impact on restorative program. Emphasize how this will help them provide care and treat residents. Explain benefits of group treatment versus individual sessions, emphasizing efficiency and effectiveness.
- Detail what the restorative aides role will be and what is expected of them. Communicate roles in exercise and cognitive groups, offer to allow them to lead groups, and present facilitation role of the recreation therapist.
- Review schedule and calendar of daily program.
- Seek ideas for activities and groups, as well as participants. Review current caseload and present information on other residents being considered for program.
- Provide training on cofacilitation, verbal cueing, and group dynamics. May do this ongoing or in groups rather than in educational session.
- Answer questions about the impact on residents not involved and how it will affect other departments. Present plan for inclusion of these residents into general recreation program instead of small group program previously offered.

Nurse's Aides

Presented by Recreation Therapist and Recreation Therapy Director on each Nursing unit

- Provide overview of Innovations program, including its purpose, participants, and the reasons for the new program. Explain benefits to residents and nursing staff.
- Discuss with CNAs the importance of having residents up and ready. Ask for assistance with transportation if resident ready after group begins.
- Present how Innovations will improve function and thus help residents and CNAs in activities of daily living.
- Remind CNAs to encourage residents to be as independent as possible to continue residents' functional levels. Explain how CNAs can carry-over tasks being completed in Innovations to improve functioning.
- Ask CNAs to provide assistance by making referrals when changes or declines are noted in physical, cognitive or social functioning. Explain system for communicating these issues.
- Ask CNAs for input into residents for Innovations. Present list of residents being considered with reasoning for involvement.

- Answer questions about the impact on residents not involved and how it will affect other departments. Present plan for inclusion of these residents into general recreation program instead of small group program previously offered.

Nurses

Presented by Recreation Therapist and Recreation Therapy Director during monthly in-service

- Provide overview of Innovations program, including its purpose, participants, and the reasons for the new program.
- Discuss the importance of CNAs having residents up and ready, and of Nurses to have treatments completed and medications passed. Illustrate how interruptions affect residents' involvement.
- Educate about referral process, including location of forms and ways to communicate concerns or problems.
- Answer questions about the impact on residents not involved and how it will affect other departments. Present plan for inclusion of these residents into general recreation program instead of small group program previously offered.

Therapy Staff

Presented by Recreation Therapist and Recreation Therapy Director during meeting

- Provide overview of Innovations program, including its purpose, participants, and the reasons for the new program.
- Educate about the referral process. Identify how therapists can communicate problems or ideas to new participants. Discuss notification when resident is picked up or discharged by therapy staff.
- Explain availability of groups for use as group cotreatments. May need to present the benefits of group treatment to residents and staff, including effectiveness and efficiency.
- Answer questions about the impact on residents not involved and how it will affect other departments. Present plan for inclusion of these residents into general recreation program instead of small group program previously offered.

APPENDIX F

SAMPLE CALENDAR

Monday	9:45 10:30	Exercise Table games
Tuesday	9:45 10:30 11:00	Exercise Communication Mobility group
Wednesday	9:45 10:30	Exercise Cooking
Thursday	9:45 10:30 11:00	Exercise Reminiscing Mobility group
Friday	9:45 10:30	Exercise Cognitive group

APPENDIX G

DAY-TO-DAY OPERATIONS

Notification of whom is in group

- Done weekly
- Signs posted on bathroom doors in the rooms of residents involved
- Sheet with the names of participants posted in the CNA charting book
- Verbal reminders given daily
- Reminder sheet given to therapy department

Gather participants

Group begins

- Introduction of staff
- Introduction of residents
- Introduction to the activity
- Activity begins and ends

Feedback

- From residents
- To residents

Disperse group

Evaluation

- How did the group do?
- Did the activity flow?
- Was the activity appropriate for the functional abilities of residents?
- Did the activity work on identified goals?
- Were there any problems?
- What could be done differently next time to make it better?

Documentation

- Daily participation
- Progress towards goal
- Level of involvement (active or passive)

Communication

Between recreation therapy, restorative nursing, nursing, and therapy

- Problems
- Issues
- Reminders
- Weekly list
- Suggestions for new participants

APPENDIX H

SAMPLE CARE PLAN GOALS

Strength

- Resident will demonstrate increased strength as evidenced by lifting a 1-pound weight to shoulder height 3 times during Innovations without complaints of weakness 3 times per week.
- Resident will demonstrate increased strength in both lower extremities, standing with walker and moderate assistance from staff to complete tasks for 1 minute 3 times per week.

Endurance

- Resident will increase in endurance, tolerating 30 minutes of exercise during Innovations without signs, symptoms, or complaints of fatigue 3 times per week.
- Resident will demonstrate increased endurance, ambulating with walker 75 feet without complaints of fatigue 3 times per week.

Range of motion

- Resident will demonstrate increased range of motion in right shoulder as evidenced by extending right arm to complete tasks with no physical assistance 1 time in each group.
- Resident will demonstrate increased use of left lower extremity as evidenced by utilizing left leg to complete tasks with cues 50% of the time.

Fine motor skills

- Resident will demonstrate improved fine motor abilities, being able to button 6 buttons independently 100% of the time.

Maintenance of physical functioning

- Resident will maintain current level of functional abilities as evidenced by exercising in Innovations program 5 times per week. and by walking to and from the lobby independently daily.

Communication

- Resident will demonstrate increased verbal interaction by responding to questions with fewer than 2 cues 3 times per week.

Sequencing

- Resident will demonstrate increased sequencing as evidenced by completing sequencing tasks accurately with minimal assistance 50% of the time.

Problem solving

- Resident will display improved problem solving, answering everyday problem situations with 75% accuracy 3 times per week.

APPENDIX I

SAMPLE DOOR SIGN

Posted on bathroom door or bulletin board by resident's bed
Use bright colored paper to catch the eye of staff

Master

______________________ is
scheduled to be in therapy in
the Hall 300 dining room
____
______________________________.

Sample

Mrs. Cornelia Brown is
scheduled to be in therapy in
the Hall 300 dining room
between 9:45 and 10:15
Monday through Friday.

APPENDIX J

SAMPLE WEEKLY NOTICE

REMINDER! The following people are scheduled for "Innovations" groups at the following times. Please have them *dressed, toileted, and ready for therapy in the hall dining room by the time indicated below.* See recreation therapy with questions. Thank you!

	9:45	**10:15**	**11:00**
Monday			
Tuesday			
Wednesday			
Thursday			
Friday			

Each unit is given a copy with only their residents listed. The unit supervisors and nurses each receive one. A copy is placed in the CNA daily treatment book. Copies with all residents listed are given to recreation therapy, restorative nursing, and therapy.

APPENDIX K

SAMPLE NURSING MEMO

TO: Nursing Unit Supervisors
RE: Innovations Groups

Please consider the long-term care residents on your hallway and let me know if they have shown any recent declines in mobility (ambulation or wheelchair), cognitive functioning, or physical functioning. Please indicate who and exactly what declines have been noted. Include any changes noted on most recent Quality Indicator report.

Please return by Friday so these residents can be placed into Innovations for the following week. Thanks!

NAME	DECLINE

APPENDIX L

AUDIT

Purpose
To ensure that Innovations is providing effective, quality services to improve or maintain residents' functional abilities.

Group types
Classify each group in ONE of the following categories

Physical Groups	Frequency	Cognitive Groups	Frequency
UE exercise		Current events	
LE exercise		Reminiscing	
UE/LE exercises		Problem solving	
Weights/dowels		Card games	
Active games		Word games	
Ambulation		Orientation	
Other		Other	

Service
________ Number of treatment minutes provided during the month
________ Number of groups held during the month
________ Number of residents involved in Innovations during the month

Documentation
________ ROM assessments reviewed

Referrals
________ Referrals received during the month
________ Referrals accepted during the month
________ Percent accepted of those received

Comments/Observations

APPENDIX M

INNOVATIONS EVALUATION

We are seeking feedback on the Innovations program. Your responses will be kept confidential. Recreation therapy staff involved in the provision of Innovations will not see individual comments, but a summary of your answers.

Please rate the following statements based on this scale
1: Strongly Disagree 2: Disagree 3: Neutral 4: Agree 5: Strongly Agree

____ 1. The activities/tasks in Innovations are appropriate to accomplish the functional goals of the program.

____ 2. There is enough variety in the activities and tasks in Innovations.

____ 3. The groups are lead effectively.

____ 4. Communication about expectations and activities is sufficient and appropriate for staff to understand.

____ 5. Directions are easy for residents to understand and follow.

____ 6. Conversation occurring during the group involves residents.

____ 7. Residents are provided cues and encouragement as needed.

____ 8. Recreation therapy staff have appropriate knowledge of therapeutic activities, cueing, physical interventions and leadership techniques.

____ 9. Innovations is well-organized and runs smoothly.

____ 10. Innovations is a worthwhile program that accomplishes the program's goals of improving or maintaining residents' functional abilities.

Additional Comments

APPENDIX N

PHYSICIAN ORDERS

Treatment areas for physician orders

Endurance	Range of motion
Strengthening	Concentration
Balance	Problem solving
Fine motor coordination	Sequencing
Gross motor coordination	Memory
Orientation	Social skills
Attention	Lifestyle adjustment
Comprehension	Coping

Physician orders

- Frequency and duration of treatment, as well as specific modalities should be included. If a resident is going to be involved in group treatment, this must be included in the physician orders.
- It is recommended that orders be written on forms already used by the facility to obtain physician orders to prevent confusion.
- Prior to obtaining physician orders, the recreation therapist may need to provide education to the doctors on the benefits and impact of recreation therapy.
- Be sure to include the patient's name on the orders.

Sample orders

Physical order
Recreation therapist to treat resident in Innovations group program for strengthening and endurance 5 times per week QD x 4 weeks.

Cognitive order
Recreation therapist to treat resident for attention to task and problem solving 3 times per week QD x 2 weeks.

BIBLIOGRAPHY

Borg, B. and Bruce, M. A. G. (1991). *The group system: The therapeutic activity group in occupational therapy*. Thorofare, NJ: SLACK, Inc.

Brookcrest Christian Nursing Home. (1997). *Recreation Therapy Department Statement of Purpose*.

Cole, M. B. (1993). Group dynamics in occupational therapy: The theoretical basis and practical application of group treatment. Thorofare, NJ: SLACK, Inc.

Edginton, C. R., Hanson, C. J., and Edginton, S. R. (1992). *Leisure programming: Concepts, trends, and professional practice* (2nd ed.). Dubuque, IA: Brown and Benchmark.

Garner, G. O. (1994). *Careers in social and rehabilitation services*. Lincolnwood, IL: NTC Publishing Group.

Greenblatt, F. S. (1988). *Therapeutic recreation for long-term care facilities*. New York, NY: Human Sciences Press, Inc.

Howe, M. C. and Schwartzberg, S. L. (1995). *A functional approach to group work in occupational therapy* (2nd ed.). Philadelphia, PA: JB Lippincott Company.

Lewis, C. B. (1985). *Aging—the health care challenge: An interdisciplinary approach to assessment and rehabilitative management of the elderly*. Philadelphia, PA: F. A. Davis Company.

Lewis, C. B and Bottomley, J. M. (1995). *Geriatric physical therapy: A clinical approach*. Nowalk, CT: Appleton and Lange.

Peterson, C. A. and Gunn, S. L. (1984). *Therapeutic recreation program design: Principles and procedures*. Englewood Cliffs, NJ: Prentice-Hall, Inc.

Russoniello, C. V. (1992, August/September). More than simple recreation. *REHAB Management*, 32–37.

U. S. Department of Health and Human Services: Public Health Service, Agency for Health Care Policy and Research. (1996). Post-stroke rehabilitation: Clinical practice guidelines. Gaithersburg, MD: Aspen Publishers, Inc.

Weiler, J. (1998, August 10). All together now: Group treatment can work for SNFs. *ADVANCE for Physical Therapists and Physical Therapy Assistants*, 28–31.

BOOKS BY VENTURE PUBLISHING

The A•B•Cs of Behavior Change: Skills for Working With Behavior Problems in Nursing Homes
by Margaret D. Cohn, Michael A. Smyer, and Ann L. Horgas

Activity Experiences and Programming within Long-Term Care
by Ted Tedrick and Elaine R. Green

The Activity Gourmet
by Peggy Powers

Advanced Concepts for Geriatric Nursing Assistants
by Carolyn A. McDonald

Adventure Programming
edited by John C. Miles and Simon Priest

Assessment: The Cornerstone of Activity Programs
by Ruth Perschbacher

Behavior Modification in Therapeutic Recreation: An Introductory Manual
by John Datillo and William D. Murphy

Benefits of Leisure
edited by B. L. Driver, Perry J. Brown, and George L. Peterson

Benefits of Recreation Research Update
by Judy M. Sefton and W. Kerry Mummery

Beyond Bingo: Innovative Programs for the New Senior
by Sal Arrigo, Jr., Ann Lewis, and Hank Mattimore

Beyond Bingo 2: More Innovative Programs for the New Senior
by Sal Arrigo, Jr.

Both Gains and Gaps: Feminist Perspectives on Women's Leisure
by Karla Henderson, M. Deborah Bialeschki, Susan M. Shaw, and Valeria J. Freysinger

Dimensions of Choice: A Qualitative Approach to Recreation, Parks, and Leisure Research
by Karla A. Henderson

Diversity and the Recreation Profession: Organizational Perspectives
edited by Maria T. Allison and Ingrid E. Schneider

Effective Management in Therapeutic Recreation Service
by Gerald S. O'Morrow and Marcia Jean Carter

Everything From A to Y: The Zest Is up to You! Older Adult Activities for Every Day of the Year
by Nancy R. Cheshire and Martha L. Kenney

Evaluating Leisure Services: Making Enlightened Decisions, Second Edition
by Karla A. Henderson and M. Deborah Bialeschki

The Evolution of Leisure: Historical and Philosophical Perspectives
by Thomas Goodale and Geoffrey Godbey

Experience Marketing: Strategies for the New Millennium
by Ellen L. O'Sullivan and Kathy J. Spangler

Facilitation Techniques in Therapeutic Recreation
by John Dattilo

File o' Fun: A Recreation Planner for Games & Activities, Third Edition
by Jane Harris Ericson and Diane Ruth Albright

The Game and Play Leader's Handbook: Facilitating Fun and Positive Interaction
by Bill Michaelis and John M. O'Connell

The Game Finder—A Leader's Guide to Great Activities
by Annette C. Moore

Getting People Involved in Life and Activities: Effective Motivating Techniques
by Jeanne Adams

Glossary of Recreation Therapy and Occupational Therapy
by David R. Austin

Great Special Events and Activities
by Annie Morton, Angie Prosser, and Sue Spangler

Group Games & Activity Leadership
by Kenneth J. Bulik

Hands on! Children's Activities for Fairs, Festivals, and Special Events
by Karen L. Ramey

Inclusive Leisure Services: Responding to the Rights of People with Disabilities, Second Edition
by John Dattilo

Innovations: A Recreation Therapy Approach to Restorative Programs
by Dawn R. De Vries and Julie M. Lake

Internships in Recreation and Leisure Services: A Practical Guide for Students, Second Edition
by Edward E. Seagle, Jr., Ralph W. Smith, and Lola M. Dalton

Interpretation of Cultural and Natural Resources
by Douglas M. Knudson, Ted T. Cable, and Larry Beck

Intervention Activities for At-Risk Youth
by Norma J. Stumbo

Introduction to Recreation and Leisure Services, Eighth Edition
by Karla A. Henderson, M. Deborah Bialeschki, John L. Hemingway, Jan S. Hodges, Beth D. Kivel, and H. Douglas Sessoms

Introduction to Writing Goals and Objectives: A Manual for Recreation Therapy Students and Entry-Level Professionals
by Suzanne Melcher

Leadership and Administration of Outdoor Pursuits, Second Edition
by Phyllis Ford and James Blanchard

Leadership in Leisure Services: Making a Difference, Second Edition
by Debra J. Jordan

Leisure and Leisure Services in the 21st Century
by Geoffrey Godbey

The Leisure Diagnostic Battery: Users Manual and Sample Forms
by Peter A. Witt and Gary Ellis

Leisure Education I: A Manual of Activities and Resources, Second Edition
by Norma J. Stumbo

Leisure Education II: More Activities and Resources, Second Edition
by Norma J. Stumbo

Leisure Education III: More Goal-Oriented Activities
by Norma J. Stumbo

Leisure Education IV: Activities for Individuals with Substance Addictions
by Norma J. Stumbo

Leisure Education Program Planning: A Systematic Approach, Second Edition
by John Dattilo

Leisure Education Specific Programs
by John Dattilo

Leisure in Your Life: An Exploration, Fifth Edition
by Geoffrey Godbey

Leisure Services in Canada: An Introduction, Second Edition
by Mark S. Searle and Russell E. Brayley

Leisure Studies: Prospects for the Twenty-First Century
edited by Edgar L. Jackson and Thomas L. Burton

The Lifestory Re-Play Circle: A Manual of Activities and Techniques
by Rosilyn Wilder

Models of Change in Municipal Parks and Recreation: A Book of Innovative Case Studies
edited by Mark E. Havitz

More Than a Game: A New Focus on Senior Activity Services
by Brenda Corbett

Nature and the Human Spirit: Toward an Expanded Land Management Ethic
edited by B. L. Driver, Daniel Dustin, Tony Baltic, Gary Elsner, and George Peterson

Outdoor Recreation Management: Theory and Application, Third Edition
by Alan Jubenville and Ben Twight

Planning Parks for People, Second Edition
by John Hultsman, Richard L. Cottrell, and Wendy Z. Hultsman

The Process of Recreation Programming Theory and Technique, Third Edition
by Patricia Farrell and Herberta M. Lundegren

Programming for Parks, Recreation, and Leisure Services: A Servant Leadership Approach
by Donald G. DeGraaf, Debra J. Jordan, and Kathy H. DeGraaf

Protocols for Recreation Therapy Programs
edited by Jill Kelland, along with the Recreation Therapy Staff at Alberta Hospital Edmonton

Quality Management: Applications for Therapeutic Recreation
edited by Bob Riley

A Recovery Workbook: The Road Back from Substance Abuse
by April K. Neal and Michael J. Taleff

Recreation and Leisure: Issues in an Era of Change, Third Edition
edited by Thomas Goodale and Peter A. Witt

Recreation Economic Decisions: Comparing Benefits and Costs, Second Edition
by John B. Loomis and Richard G. Walsh

Recreation for Older Adults: Individual and Group Activities
by Judith A. Elliott and Jerold E. Elliott

Recreation Programming and Activities for Older Adults
by Jerold E. Elliott and Judith A. Sorg-Elliott

Reference Manual for Writing Rehabilitation Therapy Treatment Plans
by Penny Hogberg and Mary Johnson

Research in Therapeutic Recreation: Concepts and Methods
edited by Marjorie J. Malkin and Christine Z. Howe

Simple Expressions: Creative and Therapeutic Arts for the Elderly in Long-Term Care Facilities
by Vicki Parsons

A Social History of Leisure Since 1600
by Gary Cross

A Social Psychology of Leisure
by Roger C. Mannell and Douglas A. Kleiber

Steps to Successful Programming: A Student Handbook to Accompany Programming for Parks, Recreation, and Leisure Services
by Donald G. DeGraaf, Debra J. Jordan, and Kathy H. DeGraaf

Stretch Your Mind and Body: Tai Chi as an Adaptive Activity
by Duane A. Crider and William R. Klinger

Therapeutic Activity Intervention with the Elderly: Foundations and Practices
by Barbara A. Hawkins, Marti E. May, and Nancy Brattain Rogers

Therapeutic Recreation: Cases and Exercises, Second Edition
by Barbara C. Wilhite and M. Jean Keller

Therapeutic Recreation in the Nursing Home
by Linda Buettner and Shelley L. Martin

Therapeutic Recreation Protocol for Treatment of Substance Addictions
by Rozanne W. Faulkner

Tourism and Society: A Guide to Problems and Issues
by Robert W. Wyllie

A Training Manual for Americans with Disabilities Act Compliance in Parks and Recreation Settings
by Carol Stensrud

Venture Publishing, Inc.
1999 Cato Avenue
State College, PA 16801
Phone: (814) 234-4561
Fax: (814) 234–1651